S0-ASQ-869

angston-George, Rebecca
he women's rights
novement : then and now
2018]
3305242582587
a   07/11/18

✳ Smithsonian

THE WOMEN'S RIGHTS MOVEMENT

THEN AND NOW

BY REBECCA LANGSTON-GEORGE

CONSULTANTS:
ELLEN NANNEY, LICENSING MANAGER, AND
KEALY GORDON, PRODUCT DEVELOPMENT MANAGER,
SMITHSONIAN INSTITUTION

CAPSTONE PRESS
a capstone imprint

Smithsonian is published by Capstone Press,
1710 Roe Crest Drive, North Mankato, Minnesota 56003
www.mycapstone.com

Copyright © 2018 by Capstone Press, a Capstone imprint. All rights reserved.
No part of this publication may be reproduced in whole or in part, or stored in a
retrieval system, or transmitted in any form or by any means, electronic, mechanical,
photocopying, recording, or otherwise, without written permission of the publisher.

The name of the Smithsonian Institution and the sunburst logo
are registered trademarks of the Smithsonian Institution.
For more information, please visit www.si.edu.

Library of Congress Cataloging-in-Publication Data
Cataloging-in-publication information is on file with the Library of Congress.
ISBN 978-1-5435-0386-9 (library binding)
ISBN 978-1-5435-0390-6 (paperback)
ISBN 978-1-5435-0394-4 (ebook pdf)

Editorial Credits
Michelle Bisson, editor; Russell Griesmer, designer; Svetlana Zhurkin, media
researcher; Laura Manthe production specialist

Dedication: For my sister, Nancy Tiffany, who knew her rights,
stood her ground, and demanded change.

Photo Credits
Getty Images: Bettmann, 21, 31, Denver Post, 39, Don Carl Steffen, cover (top right),
1 (bottom), H. Armstrong Roberts, 4, New York Times/Don Hogan Charles, 27, Photo
Archives/New York Post/Anthony Calvacca, 12, The LIFE Picture Collection/Alfred
Eisenstaedt, 15, The LIFE Picture Collection/John Olson, 7, The New York Historical
Society/Eugene Gordon, 22; Library of Congress, 16, 42; Newscom: AdMedia/
CNP/Ron Sachs, 57, CNP/Arnie Sachs, 49, Everett Collection, 18, 28, Glasshouse
Images, 10, Jeff Malet Photography, 55, KRT/File, 24, MCT/J.M. Eddins, Jr., 32, MCT/
Minneapolis Star Tribune/Richard Sennott, 47, Richard B. Levine, 45, Splash News/
Corbis, 37, World History Archive, 9; Shutterstock: a katz, 41, Aspen Photo, 36,
blvdone, cover (left), 1 (top), Creatista, 53, Evan El-Amin, 52, GaudiLab, 50, Joseph
Sohm, 56
Design Elements by Capstone and Shutterstock

Printed in the United States of America.
010844S18

TABLE OF CONTENTS

The stay-at-home mom was the 1960s ideal.

CHAPTER 1

THE FIGHT FOR RIGHTS: A NEW DAY DAWNS

What was a woman's life like in the early 1960s before the women's movement? Images from popular TV shows and magazines of the time would have us believe all stay-at-home mothers wore heels and pearls to vacuum. When they weren't cleaning, they attended PTA meetings and drove their children to Cub Scouts. At dinnertime they donned frilly aprons and entertained their husband's boss at dinner parties. It sounds pretty phony, right? But in 1960, the perfect mother and housewife was a popular cultural symbol. Many women tried to fit that mold.

The average woman in 1960 married at age 20. She had two or three children (2.3 to be exact). Only 38 percent of women worked outside the home compared to 83 percent of men. So statistics do indicate a large number of women in 1960 probably did stay home and raise children rather than work. While being a housewife was the ideal put forth by TV and magazines, many women found it unfulfilling. They wondered if there wasn't more to life. In the groundbreaking book, *The Feminist Mystique*, author Betty Friedan called this frustration "the problem with no name."

This frustration wasn't limited to housewives. The minority of women who worked outside the home were also frustrated. They received less pay and fewer promotions than men. The Presidential Commission on the Status of Women, started by President John F. Kennedy in 1961, confirmed this discrimination. In 1963 the Equal Pay Act was passed. It outlawed paying women less than men for doing the same job. But in reality, the law had very little effect. Employers got around it by dividing similar jobs into men's jobs and women's jobs with different titles and different salaries. Or they simply didn't allow women to apply for some jobs. So women became even more frustrated.

Years earlier women's frustration had changed history. What is now called the first wave of feminism resulted in the passage of the 19th Amendment, giving women the right to vote, starting in 1920. Though an earlier generation of women had earned them the vote, women still didn't have rights equal to men. The second wave of feminism took root in this frustration and inequality. The women's movement of the 1960s and 1970s sprang up alongside the civil rights movement, antiwar protests, and demonstrations to protect the environment. It was a time when large numbers of people rose up to challenge society's expectations and question authority.

The women who made up the movement were many and came from all walks of life. Former first lady Eleanor Roosevelt served on President Kennedy's Presidential Commission on the Status of Women until her death in 1962. Pauli Murray, a key lawyer in the civil rights movement, played an important role on the commission and later organizations.

Women marched down Fifth Avenue in New York City in 1970 to commemorate the 50th anniversary of the ratification of the 19th Amendment, which gave women the right to vote.

Journalist Gloria Steinem went undercover to expose the exploitation of women who worked as "bunnies" in Playboy Clubs and took the cause of women's liberation to the media. Shirley Chisholm dared to run as America's first black presidential candidate.

Lesser-known women were equally important, with flight attendants, teachers, and others challenging laws and demanding their rights by filing lawsuits. It was a movement of many voices, a sea of small and large demonstrations and organizations.

One group was the National Organization for Women (NOW). It was born under the leadership of Betty Friedan, Pauli Murray, Shirley Chisholm, and others. NOW organized the most visible display of the women's movement at the time. The Strike for Equality occurred on the 50th anniversary of the ratification of the 19th Amendment. On August 26, 1970, Friedan, Steinem, and thousands of other women marched down Fifth Avenue in New York City. Approximately 50,000 women went on strike for one day to demonstrate in similar marches throughout the country. Participating women walked away from their jobs for the day to protest unequal wages. Housewives refused to cook or clean at home. NOW organizers demanded equal opportunities in employment and education, government-funded childcare centers, and unrestricted abortion rights.

The second wave of feminism got a lot of media coverage and brought the inequality of the sexes out into the open. As a result, heightened awareness and new laws brought about some positive changes in education and employment. Women had come a long way, but there was still a long way to go.

THE FIRST WOMAN'S RIGHTS CONVENTION

The first Woman's Rights Convention was held in Seneca Falls, New York, July 19 and 20, 1848. It kicked off the first wave of feminism that concluded with women getting the vote in 1920. It was organized by Elizabeth Cady Stanton, Jane Hunt, Mary Ann M'Clintock, Martha Coffin Wright, and Lucretia Mott. Amid the declarations and resolutions put forth, Stanton proposed a resolution calling for women to secure the right to vote. Some of her fellow organizers felt this was asking for too much, but abolitionist Frederick Douglass, who was present in the audience, supported her. None of the organizers would live to cast a ballot 72 years later.

THE FIRST CONVENTION

EVER CALLED TO DISCUSS THE

Civil and Political Rights of Women,

SENECA FALLS, N. Y., JULY 19, 20, 1848.

___

WOMAN'S RIGHTS CONVENTION.

___

A Convention to discuss the social, civil, and religious condition and rights of woman will be held in the Wesleyan Chapel, at Seneca Falls, N. Y., on Wednesday and Thursday, the 19th and 20th of July current; commencing at 10 o'clock A. M. During the first day the meeting will be exclusively for women, who are earnestly invited to attend. The public generally are invited to be present on the second day, when Lucretia Mott, of Philadelphia, and other ladies and gentlemen, will address the Convention.*

___

*This call was published in the *Seneca County Courier*, July 14, 1848, without any signatures. The movers of this Convention, who drafted the call, the declaration and resolutions were Elizabeth Cady Stanton, Lucretia Mott, Martha C. Wright, Mary Ann McClintock, and Jane C. Hunt.

Many women replaced male factory workers during WWII.

What was it like for women in the early United States? What brought about the need for a feminist movement?

Until the last third of the 1800s, the U.S. economy was mostly based on farming. Women helped to grow, harvest, and preserve food alongside their husbands and family members. Few women held outside jobs. As the economy shifted from agriculture to industry, factories needed cheap labor, especially in urban areas. Women were hired to sew clothing and assemble light goods for lower wages than most men would accept. Higher-paying jobs were reserved for men. Most employers believed women couldn't handle tough physical labor. Later, during World War II when men were shipped overseas to fight, factories faced labor shortages. Women were brought in to manufacture heavy goods like planes. When the war ended, so did most of these jobs. Returning soldiers resumed the jobs they had left behind, putting many women out of work. Women stayed home and the U.S. experienced a baby boom, creating a culture in which women were expected to keep house and raise a family. Why, women began to wonder, couldn't they enjoy both a family and a job plus have the same rights as men? The women's movement, which had ebbed after the passage of the 19th Amendment, came roaring back to life.

EQUAL EMPLOYMENT RIGHTS

One of the most important demands of the women's movement is equal pay. In 1960 women made 40 percent less than men for comparable jobs. More than five decades after the Equal Pay Act of 1963, many women still make less than men in similar jobs. The difference is biggest in the legal field, with women earning about 57 cents for every dollar a man earns. Construction has the smallest pay gap, with females earning 91 percent of what men make.

In 1967 women across the country protested against sex discrimination in hiring.

How can companies pay different amounts for the same work? First, there are many loopholes in the act, so it doesn't apply to all jobs. For example, executive jobs, such as the president of a company, aren't covered in the act. In addition, some companies do not have set salaries for each position, so they can offer different people different amounts.

Until 1973 some companies paid different amounts for the same work by segregating jobs by gender. Job openings were advertised in the newspaper in a "want ads" section. A company might list the same exact job under men's jobs and women's jobs. The only difference might be that the listing under the heading "men's jobs" offered a larger salary. Some people defended this, claiming men had families to support so they needed a higher salary. Want ad segregation by race had been outlawed eight years earlier. But the NOW chapter in Pittsburgh, Pennsylvania, had to battle the *Pittsburgh Press* newspaper all the way to the Supreme Court to get gender segregation abolished.

Job listings discriminated in other ways as well. A want ad for United Air Lines stewardesses (flight attendants) in 1966 required applicants to be single women, at least 20 years old, and between 5'2" and 5'9" in height. Wearing contacts was "acceptable." The ad, which clearly discriminates against married women, short and tall women, and those wearing glasses, proudly proclaims at the bottom "Equal Opportunity Employer." This was standard practice for all airlines at the time.

Airlines also had strict weight requirements for stewardesses.

They were constantly weighed and measured. Stewardesses who got married were immediately fired. And it was one job where men were not welcome until several years later. The airlines wanted young, pretty, single "girls" to serve male business travelers.

Even companies that hired married women, or allowed women to remain employed after marriage, often wouldn't tolerate pregnancies. It was not unusual for a company to fire women who became pregnant. In other cases women such as Jo Carol LaFleur were forced to take unpaid maternity leave whether they wanted to or not. In 1971, LaFleur, a teacher, was required to take leave without pay five months before giving birth. She wasn't allowed to return until the start of the school semester in which her child was at least 3 months old.

While some employers did not tolerate women marrying or having babies, they often ignored men sexually harassing women in the workplace. Sexual harassment is unwanted sexual attention. It can involve words, physical contact, or showing unwanted pictures. Before 1978 an employee whose boss touched her inappropriately or made crude comments often had nowhere to turn for legal help.

EQUAL EDUCATION RIGHTS

Women didn't just face discrimination in the workplace; they faced similar problems trying to get an education. During the homemaker culture of the late 1950s and 1960s, college enrollment and college graduation rates for women dropped. A popular joke on college campuses then was that females went to college

Until 1967 Harvard University admitted only men.
Women went to the neighboring Radcliffe College.

MARGARET SANGER

Nurse, writer, and social reformer Margaret Sanger made it her life's work to ensure women had access to contraceptives. Sanger saw firsthand the effect of repeated unwanted pregnancies on women's lives. Childbirth complications led to high death rates for young women. Sanger wrote magazine articles on sex education in 1915. She opened the first birth control clinic in the U.S. in 1916. Five years later, in 1921, she founded the American Birth Control League, which would eventually be known as Planned Parenthood. Contraceptives such as condoms, as well as literature about contraception, were illegal in the U.S. because of the Comstock Law. This law, passed in 1873, classified these items as obscene. Sanger was arrested for distributing contraceptives under the Comstock Law. Still she persisted. Sanger is credited with helping arrange funding in 1953 for Gregory Pincus' research while he developed the oral contraceptive known as "the pill."

to get an Mrs. degree. And those who dropped out to marry were getting an advanced degree called a PhT (putting husband through college degree).

Cultural expectations weren't the only college roadblocks. Some colleges had higher admission standards for women than men. A woman had to have a higher grade point average than a man to apply for many graduate programs. Even worse, universities often put a limit on the number of women they would accept. Some universities, especially the elite Ivy League ones, refused to admit women at all until the 1970s. Supreme Court Justice Ruth Bader Ginsburg was one of countless women who faced discrimination in education. Her law professor demanded to know why she and the other eight females in a Harvard Law School class of 500 students should be allowed to take seats that belonged to men. And while Justice Ginsburg graduated first in her class, she was denied a clerk's job with Supreme Court Justice Felix Frankfurter. The justice did not wish to have a woman work for him. In fact, Ginsburg, the highest-ranking student of the country's best law school, had great difficulty finding a job.

Discrimination wasn't restricted to universities; it occurred at all levels of education. High school girls were usually not allowed to take classes in woodworking or automobile repair; instead, they were encouraged or required to take sewing and home economics. Science and math were often regarded as boys' subjects, resulting in teachers discouraging girls from pursuing these fields. The inequality reached all the way to the gym, where most school athletics were reserved exclusively for boys.

PAULI MURRAY

Anna Pauline Murray was a champion for both civil rights and women's rights. In 1940 she was arrested for refusing to move to the back of the bus. While Rosa Parks became famous for refusing to give up her seat to a white man on a bus, Murray took a stand 15 years sooner. She earned a law degree in 1944 and later wrote an important civil rights book: *States' Laws on Race and Color*. President John F. Kennedy appointed her to his Commission on the Status of Women in 1963, and she was a cofounder of NOW (National Organization for Women). Later in life she became an Episcopal priest. In fact, she was the first female African American to do so. As a black feminist transgender person, Murray truly fought for equal rights for all of us.

HEALTH CARE RIGHTS

Another principle of the women's movement is a woman's right to make her own health decisions. Until contraceptives were available, women had little control over their own futures. They were likely to be pregnant time after time if they were sexually active. Contraceptives allowed women to plan much more reliably when and whether they would bear children. The birth control pill, introduced in 1960, radically changed women's lives. The ability to control childbirth gave women the freedom to work, get an education, and support themselves. Yet laws and religious beliefs prohibited or limited contraception. In June 1965 the Supreme Court ruled it was unlawful to prohibit married couples from using contraceptives in *Griswold v.*

Connecticut. But it wasn't until March 1972 that the *Eisenstadt v. Baird* case legalized contraceptives for unmarried women in all 50 states. Even today there are questions about whether an employer's health care plan must cover contraceptives.

Perhaps the most controversial goal of the women's movement is a woman's right to terminate a pregnancy. Abortion was, with few exceptions, illegal throughout the country. If a woman wanted to end a pregnancy she had to rely on dangerous, illegal procedures. In 1973 the Supreme Court decided in *Roe v. Wade* that women had the right to terminate a pregnancy in its early stages and in some situations into the late stage of pregnancy.

DIVERSE VOICES WITHIN THE MOVEMENT

After the *Roe v. Wade* decision, there was a split in the women's movement between the pro-choice feminists and the anti-abortion feminists that exists to the present day. Those who are pro-choice promote a woman's right to choose an abortion. Those who are not support the protection of all unborn fetuses; some believe abortion is appropriate only in rare cases, such as when a woman's life is at stake.

There have been other divisions within the movement as well. Women of color had to struggle with both racial discrimination and gender discrimination. Some saw the 1960s women's movement as an organization for white, middle-aged, middle-class women. Certainly, many women of color were involved in the second wave and played important roles. Others, understandably, felt their loyalty belonged primarily to the civil rights movement.

Homosexual women also struggled to find their voice within the women's movement. Some in the movement, such as Betty Friedan, didn't think the unique issues lesbian women faced were mainstream feminist issues. Friedan said the topic made her "uneasy." Homosexuality was a controversial topic at the time. The failure to recognize all women's rights as important led to some homosexual women branching off to form their own organizations.

Even age brought out different viewpoints. Younger women in the late 1960s and early 1970s had different views on marriage and relationships than older women. The older women were sometimes scandalized by the younger women's desire not to marry, but rather to live together with a partner.

Despite all their various viewpoints, one thing all the women agreed upon was that things had to change for the better for women.

Elinor Griswold, executive director of Planned Parenthood, was arrested in the 1960s for providing birth control to married women.

Thousands participated in the Women's Strike for Peace and Equality in 1970.

WOMEN MAKE THEIR DEMANDS KNOWN

While the 1970 Strike for Equality is perhaps the best-known demonstration to come out of the second wave of feminism, it wasn't the first. Former child actor and feminist activist Robin Morgan organized a protest against America's annual TV ratings blockbuster, the Miss America Pageant. On September 7, 1968, picketers gathered outside the pageant studio in Atlantic City. Inside, the contestants strolled the catwalk in swimsuits and bouffant hairdos, hoping to win the crown. Outside, demonstrators led a sheep down the boardwalk to show that the pageant judged women like farmers judged animals at the fair. Some protesters smuggled a "Women's Liberation" banner inside the auditorium and hung it from the balcony. Marchers waved signs and chanted. They set up a trash can in which women could throw away high heels, makeup, curlers, and other items associated with society's pressure to attain its standards of feminine beauty.

Women also targeted another popular cultural icon of the time: the *Ladies' Home Journal* magazine. Full of articles on housekeeping, cooking, and home decorating, the magazine catered to traditional housewives.

On the morning of March 18, 1970, under the leadership of author and journalist Susan Brownmiller, a hundred women marched into the office of John Mack Carter, the magazine's editor in chief. They staged a sit-in and presented their list of demands. They wanted the magazine to stop running ads they felt degraded women and stop stories that promoted traditional roles for women.

The magazine, they insisted, had to begin providing free childcare for all its employees. Most importantly, they wanted the magazine to allow the protesters to write the content for an upcoming issue. After an 11-hour stand-off, Carter compromised by allowing the protesters to write an eight-page feminist insert for the August 1970 edition.

STYLE

Women also made their voices heard in the styles they wore. As society's view of women changed, women's fashion, makeup, and hairdos also changed to reflect women's new roles. Previously, employers and schools often had strict dress codes for females. Schoolgirls' dress hems had to extend below their knees. Working women were expected to wear modest makeup and conservative hairstyles. Women who worked in offices often wore a

Gloria Steinem was a major player in the women's movement.

girdle, a garter belt to hold up their nylon stockings, dresses, heels, gloves, and a hat. Pants, jeans, and shorts were never acceptable on the job or at school. In fact, Mary Tyler Moore caused a stir because her character on *The Dick Van Dyke Show*, Laura Petrie, was the first female character on TV to regularly wear pants. In real life, Lois Rabinowitz was thrown out of a New York traffic court in 1960 when she committed the "crime" of wearing pants to pay a traffic fine. Lois' husband, who had given her a ride, had to take her place and pay the fine. Apparently, Mr. Rabinowitz's pants didn't bother the judge.

With the women's movement many women began to leave behind uncomfortable garments and strict rules about what men and women could wear. Instead, they chose comfortable, practical, and more casual clothes in

"YOU DON'T OWN ME"

The women's movement even affected the music industry. Several songs about female empowerment went to the top of the charts.

You Don't Own Me, sung by Lesley Gore, reached #2 in February 1964.

Respect, by Aretha Franklin, topped the charts at #1 in June 1967.

I Am Woman, Helen Reddy's ultimate women's anthem, was #1 in December 1972.

The Pill, by country artist Loretta Lynn, reached #70 in March 1975, despite its controversial subject.

the 1970s like pants and flowing maxi dresses. Women began to wear more natural makeup styles and they left behind elaborate, hair-sprayed bouffant hairdos. Natural hair became the new beautiful. Long, flowing hair was in. Afro hairstyles gained popularity among African American women who stopped straightening their hair.

In 1960 only two of the 100 U.S. senators were women. Seventeen of the 435 members of the House of Representatives were female. With women making up only 3 percent of Congress, women's issues weren't getting the attention they deserved. Movement leaders quickly realized there were two ways to change that. First, women needed to be politically active. Not only did they need to vote, they also needed to contact their representatives, express their views, and demand change.

Also, they had to band together to get more like-minded women elected to Congress. Demonstrators put a new spin on the "Votes for Women" signs once held by suffragists. The new slogan became "Vote for a Woman."

The idea of more women in government didn't sit well with everyone. Some questioned a woman's ability to make important decisions, claiming women were too emotional to think clearly. Working women and women in politics would lead to the downfall of the family, they claimed. They still believed a woman's place was in the home.

> **Those in the movement believed in the slogan "a woman's place is in the House and Senate."**

Shirley Chisholm found her place in the House as the first black woman in Congress in 1968. Four years later she set her sights higher and campaigned unsuccessfully for the presidency in the Democratic primary of 1972. Chisholm, who once said, "If they don't give you a seat at the table, bring a folding chair," faced threats and discrimination

Shirley Chisholm announced her presidential candidacy in 1972.

even within her own party. She had to file a complaint with the Federal Communications Commission to be included in her own party's televised presidential debate. Chisholm said, "I met more discrimination as a woman than for being black." Even the organization she helped co-found, NOW, publicly supported another candidate instead of one of their own. Shirley Chisholm knew her presidential run wouldn't result in her election, but she blazed the trail for others to come, such as Barack Obama and Hillary Clinton. Chisholm said,

"The next time a woman runs, or a black, or a Jew or anyone from a group that the country is 'not ready' to elect to its highest office, I believe that he or she will be taken seriously from the start . . . I ran because somebody had to do it first. In this country everybody is supposed to be able to run for President, but that has never really been true."

Bella Abzug, a lawyer and member of NOW, was elected to the House of Representatives in 1970. Previously active in the Women's Strike for Peace in 1961, Abzug was known for wearing colorful hats.

Her mother had suggested early in life that she wear a hat to show she wasn't part of the secretarial pool in the office, but a person who was in charge. Bella herself said, "It's what's under the hat that counts."

Bella Abzug in her trademark hat

Always bold and outspoken, Abzug proposed a bill on her very first day of office to pull all U.S. troops out of Vietnam. Later, in 1974, she drafted The Equality Act, the first gay rights bill. The act sought to prohibit discrimination on the basis of sex, marital status, and sexual orientation. Both of these attempts were unsuccessful, but brought awareness to important issues.

LAWSUITS

Women also demanded change through the courts. Lawsuits focused national and community attention on issues. They helped bring about change by forcing companies to comply with the law and hitting them in the pocketbook when they didn't.

In 1970 *Newsweek* magazine decided to run a cover story on women's liberation. At the time, all writers on the *Newsweek* staff were male except for one: Lynn Povich. She got the role of junior writer only because *Newsweek* needed a woman to cover fashion. The highest job any of the other women at *Newsweek* could hope to attain was researcher. The magazine didn't believe in hiring women writers. The editors decided they needed a woman's point of view to cover the women's liberation story. So they gave the job to a woman. But the job didn't go to Lynn Povich or any of the women researchers. In fact, it wasn't given to any of the women already employed at the magazine. Instead, it went to the wife of one of the male writers. The women of *Newsweek* were furious. Forty-six of them banded together to take action. Povich contacted the Equal Employment Opportunity Commission (EEOC), and with the help of Eleanor Holmes Norton, the assistant legal director for the American Civil Liberties Union, they announced a discrimination lawsuit against *Newsweek* on the very day the women's liberation cover story ran. It took two years for *Newsweek* to agree to changes. But by 1972 *Newsweek* finally opened up writing jobs to women. Lynn Povich later became the first woman in management at *Newsweek*.

Lorena Weeks sued telephone company Southern Bell for not complying with the Equal Pay Act. She was working as a clerk when a better-paying switchman's job opened up. She applied, but was told the job was only for men because of the heavy lifting required. Weeks contacted the EEOC, stating she'd been discriminated against. Southern Bell said Georgia law prohibited women from lifting more than 30 pounds on the job and a switchman had to move a 30-pound testing machine. Weeks filed an appeal, but lost. Angry, Weeks began refusing to move her 34-pound typewriter onto her desk each morning as required, citing that same Georgia law. As a result, she was suspended for refusing to do her job. Lorena Weeks got legal help from NOW. Eventually, she won her case, got the job, and was awarded $31,000 in back pay.

In 1970 female *Newsweek* employees sued the magazine under the 1964 Civil Rights Act, charging discrimination. Women were allowed to research articles, but not to write them.

Bernice Sandler

CHAPTER 4

THE TIMES THEY ARE A-CHANGIN' (FOR THE BETTER)

The Women's Movement brought about change and progress in many ways.

EDUCATION

Many universities that were once closed to women opened their doors in the 1970s because of Title IX of the Educational Amendments Act. It says, "No person in the United States shall, on the basis of sex, be excluded from participation in, be denied the benefits of, or be subjected to discrimination under any education program or activity receiving Federal financial assistance." Fearing lawsuits and lost federal funding, most colleges lifted admissions quotas and higher entry standards for women. The number of women getting bachelor's degrees also rose.

All this educational progress might not have happened had it not been for Bernice Sandler. Known as the "Godmother of Title IX," Sandler was teaching at the University of Maryland when she was overlooked for a promotion despite being qualified. She was told that she "came on too strong for a woman."

A few months later during a job interview, she was told she wouldn't be hired because "women stayed at home when their children were sick."

PERCENT OF POPULATION WITH BACHELOR'S DEGREES

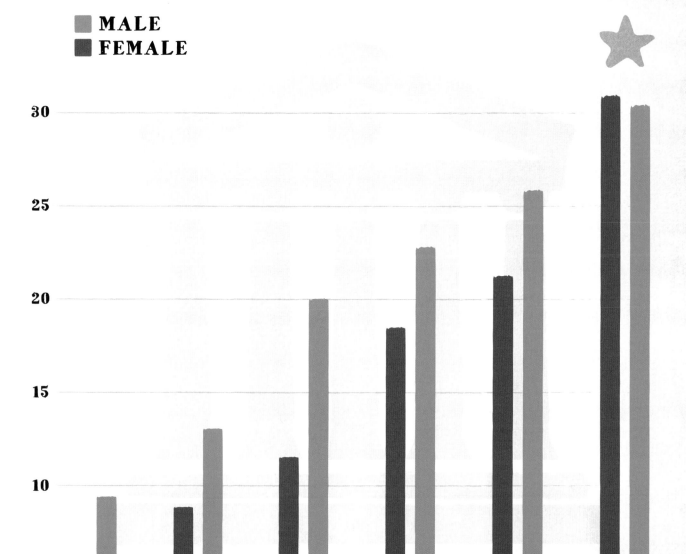

- **MALE**
- **FEMALE**

30

25

20

15

10

5

1960   1970   1980   1990   2000   2015

A counselor at an employment agency told Sandler she "wasn't really a professional, just a housewife who went back to school."

Upset and angry, Sandler began researching the laws African Americans had used to fight for civil rights. She came across a report describing President Lyndon Johnson's executive order stating federal contractors couldn't discriminate based on race or religion. There was a footnote that said the order had been expanded to forbid discrimination based on gender. Sandler worked with the Women's Equity Action League and Vincent Macaluso at the Department of Labor to bring attention to the matter. Sandler testified at Representative Edith Green's congressional hearings on discrimination in women's education and employment, but it took two years for Representative Green's Title IX to become law.

TITLE IX IMPACT ON ATHLETICS

Prior to Title IX, schools spent far less money on female sport teams and physical education than on male teams. Fewer than 300,000 high school girls in the United States participated in sports. In college the number dropped to a tenth of that, with 30,000 college women involved in sports.

Virtually everything about sports for women was unequal in those days. Schools spent 98 percent of their sports budget on males. Females got used, hand-me-down equipment. They often had to buy their own uniforms and raise money through bake sales and donations to pay for buses to take

Title IX meant that girls could fully participate in school team sports.

them to games. In some schools there were no changing rooms for girls. Female coaches were paid less than male coaches. Even practice times were unequal, with girls having to work around boys' practice times.

Title IX took several years to fully take effect, but it ushered in far more opportunities and equality for today's girls in school sports. Since it only applies to schools receiving federal funds, it has had less of an impact on professional sports.

BILLIE JEAN KING VS. BOBBY RIGGS

When 29-year-old rising women's tennis star Billie Jean King accepted 55-year-old former Wimbledon champion Bobby Riggs' challenge to play a tennis match, TV billed it as the Battle of the Sexes. Riggs' goal was to create a publicity stunt showing male athletes as superior to women. It may have also been a ploy for the past-his-prime athlete to gain some attention and a quick buck.

With comments like "Women belong in the bedroom and kitchen, in that order," he got a lot of media buzz. In fact, 90 million people tuned in to watch King and Riggs play in the Houston Astrodome on September 20, 1973. Billie Jean King knew that there was more at stake than the $100,000 prize money. When she won the match point and beat Riggs at his own game, she won respect for all female athletes.

When it comes to paid sports and Olympic sports, women still receive far less attention and money. Five players on the Women's National Soccer Team filed a wage discrimination complaint with the EEOC in 2016. Although the team brings in $18 million a year in ticket sales, advertising, and other income, the women players only earned one-fourth as much as the male soccer players.

CREDIT AND PROPERTY

There was a time when women didn't have the same right to own property as men. In the early 1970s property was often listed in the husband's name only. The wife, when she was included on the property deed, was often listed as "and spouse," rather than by name. Single women, unlike single men, had great difficulty buying property. Depending upon which state a woman lived in, it was difficult or even impossible for her to get her own credit card. Many banks wouldn't allow women to open accounts unless a husband or father was also listed on the account. Banks felt women were a bad credit risk, believing they would quit their jobs to have babies. But all that changed in 1974 when Congress passed the Depository Institutions Amendments Act. It made it illegal for banks and lenders to discriminate against women.

HEALTH CARE

Women's reproductive rights changed for the better because of the women's movement. Contraceptives are now easily available and usually covered by insurance. Free contraceptives can also be found at Planned Parenthood and free clinics. Women now have the federal right to

In the 1970s banks run by women began to open. They offered accounts and credits to women and men.

unpaid maternity leave at many jobs, and some employers offer paid leave as well. Family leave can sometimes be extended, can include time off for adoption, and can be taken by fathers as well as mothers. The Pregnancy Discrimination Act of 1978 put an end to firing or discriminating against pregnant women. As a result, unlike teacher Jo Carol LaFleur in 1971, women can't be forced to take unwanted leave because they're pregnant.

Still, a woman's right to control her own body remains a divisive topic. *Roe v. Wade* continues to be a politically charged topic. Some people want to see the Supreme Court reverse its decision. Each time a Supreme Court seat is vacant the nominee is grilled on his or her views on the case. Planned Parenthood, which provides free and inexpensive contraceptives and healthcare, has recently been threatened with "defunding." Despite what some politicians may say, there is no specific allowance for Planned Parenthood in the federal budget. Instead, Planned Parenthood receives federal reimbursements for its services when its patients use Medicaid, just as do all other participating health care providers. Medicaid is a health insurance plan for low-income people funded by the government. Should Planned Parenthood be denied Medicaid reimbursement, it would make family planning more difficult for women who don't make enough money to pay the going health insurance rates.

Women marched in support of
Planned Parenthood.

Phyllis Schlafly became famous
as an antifeminist.

Women have come a long way since the Women's Strike for Equality in 1970. Unfortunately, there is still a long way to go.

EQUAL RIGHTS AMENDMENT

The longest-running battle in the women's movement continues to be the fight to get the Equal Rights Amendment (ERA) passed. Alice Paul wrote the original text of the ERA in 1923, calling it the "Lucretia Mott Amendment" in honor of early feminist Mott. It said, "Men and women shall have equal rights throughout the United States and every place subject to its jurisdiction." Even though the wording is simple and the idea behind it seems obvious, the ERA (renamed as such in 1943) is nearly a hundred years old and still hasn't passed.

The ERA was introduced into every session of Congress from 1923 through 1972. The wording was eventually changed to, "Equality of rights under the law shall not be denied or abridged by the United States or by any state on account of sex." NOW took up the cause in 1967, vowing to fight until it passed. By 1972 the ERA was passed by both the House of Representatives and the Senate. The Senate placed a limit of seven years for states to ratify the ERA, but it was extended to June 30, 1982. In order to become the 28th Amendment to the Constitution, 38 states needed to ratify the amendment.

One woman made it her mission to make sure the ERA didn't pass. In 1972 Phyllis Schlafly founded Stop ERA, which she said stood for Stop Taking Our Privileges. Politically active, well spoken, and educated in law, Schlafly was very vocal about her opinions. In a 1972 issue of her newsletter, the *Phyllis Schlafly Report*, she wrote "Women's libbers are trying to make wives and mothers unhappy with their career, make them feel that they are 'second-class citizens' and 'abject slaves.' Women's libbers are promoting free sex instead of the 'slavery' of marriage. They are promoting Federal 'day-care centers' for babies instead of homes. They are promoting abortions instead of families."

The ERA, Schlafly claimed, would lead to women being drafted into military service, take away a woman's right NOT to work (caps are hers), deny women the right to be financially supported by her husband, and keep her babies. A lot of people believed or agreed with her. Only 35 states voted for the ERA, three short of passage. The 15 states that did not ratify the ERA before the deadline are Alabama, Arizona, Arkansas, Florida, Georgia, Illinois, Louisiana, Mississippi, Missouri, Nevada, North Carolina, Oklahoma, South Carolina, Utah, and Virginia. In 1983 and for several years after, the ERA was again introduced into every session of Congress. In 2017 Nevada became the 36th state to ratify it. That same year it was reintroduced in several of the opposing states. To date, it still hasn't passed.

EQUAL PAY

Another problem that hasn't been solved is equal pay for women. The pay gap between men and women has narrowed over the years. But women are still behind. There's even a national day that recognizes this fact. Equal Pay Day falls on a Tuesday in early April each year. Equal Pay Day for 2018 is Tuesday, April 10. Equal Pay Day demonstrates how much longer a woman has to work to earn the same amount as a man. The average woman would have to work almost 16 months (January to December of one year plus January to April of the next year) to earn the same amount a man would earn in 12 months.

Marchers gathered at the annual Equal Pay Day rally to protest the gap in pay between men and women.

The workplace is unequal in other ways as well. Women don't hold nearly as many executive jobs as men. The term "glass ceiling" is used to describe this as though there is an invisible ceiling holding women back from rising to jobs at the top. Many companies continue their tradition of secrecy about salaries, making it difficult for women who suspect discrimination to demand change.

Though the Equal Employment Opportunity Commission (EEOC) has been around since 1965 and has helped many women, it isn't the cure-all for the problem. Many complaints to the EEOC never get investigated. Others take years to process and even more years to work through the court system. In addition, lawsuits can be expensive. For women who are suing to get equal pay to begin with, it can cause financial hardships.

Part of the problem may be how our culture values different types of jobs. Society tends to place a higher worth on jobs traditionally held by men. Likewise, jobs traditionally held by women, such as teaching or nursing, are viewed as less worthy. Generally, if an occupation is mostly worked by women, it pays less.

SEXUAL HARASSMENT

Most companies now have written procedures in place for employees to report sexual harassment. They train managers to spot, identify, and correct inappropriate behavior in order to avoid lawsuits. Surprisingly, when Congress held hearings in 1981 to create guidelines about sexual harassment for the EEOC, not everyone supported the idea. Phyllis Schlafly said there was no need for regulations. "Sexual harassment on the job is not a

Lois Jenson fought and eventually won a sexual harassment suit against Eveleth Mines.

problem for a virtuous woman, except in the rarest of cases."

With victim shaming like that, it's no wonder women still hesitate to report sexual harassment. It can be very intimidating to report one's boss or coworker. Women often fear they will be labeled as troublemakers, not get promotions, or even lose their jobs—and that's because all of those things have happened to women. They may face even more harassment as their claims are investigated.

Lois Jenson complained to the Minnesota Human Rights Department in 1984 after suffering nine years of constant sexual harassment as one of the few women employed by the Eveleth Mines. The case dragged on for years and Jenson suffered from post-traumatic stress disorder. Her trial caused even more psychological damage, as she endured months of questioning about her private life and medical records. She, along with the women she worked with, was awarded only a few thousand dollars. It was little comfort since she could no longer work because of the strain. Jenson appealed the decision. In 1997, 22 years after the harassment began and 13 years after the original decision, she and 14 of her female coworkers finally split a $3.5 million settlement.

New technology has ushered in new methods of sexual harassment, making it difficult for laws to keep up with the times. The Internet has made it easy to send unwanted images through email or harass someone through social media. Electronic gadgets can be used to spy on and take pictures of those being harassed without their knowledge.

Some women have found that when they do bring sexual harassment suits the resulting math and logic don't add up. When several female employees claimed that Roger Ailes, the late Fox News chairman, harassed them, he was dismissed but given $40 million. Less than a year later, five employees claimed that Bill O'Reilly, a popular Fox News host, had harassed them. Those women were given a total of $13 million. The host and Fox News agreed to part ways, with the host receiving $25 million, nearly twice the amount his accusers received.

ANITA HILL AND CLARENCE THOMAS

One of the most famous claims of sexual harassment in the U.S. involved Supreme Court Associate Justice Clarence Thomas. When Thomas was nominated to the Supreme Court in 1991, a former coworker, Anita Hill, sent a letter to the Senate Judiciary Committee. In it, she described sexual harassment she claimed she suffered while working with Thomas. At the time, they had both worked at the Equal Employment Opportunity Commission. It was the very commission that investigated sexual harassment. Hill was called to testify at Thomas' confirmation hearing after a private interview was leaked to the press. Hill had described being sexually harassed by Thomas on the job. She claimed Thomas described pornographic movies, pestered her for dates, and rated her clothes on how sexy they were.

Despite Hill's testimony, Clarence Thomas was confirmed to the Supreme Court by an all-male Senate committee.

Women and men are now
used to sharing a workplace.

Television and magazines are likely to show today's woman juggling it all: a family, a job, and housework. If she marries at all, the average woman today marries at 25; that's five years later than the 1960s woman. She is more likely to be single than her grandmother was, with 53 percent of women age 18 or older unmarried in 2015. She has only one or two children (1.8 is the statistical average). Fifty-seven percent of women are employed. And while the number of women in the workforce has risen, the number of employed men has fallen to about 72 percent. This shows a trend toward a more even balance of men and women in the work force.

But despite the shift away from the traditional role of men as breadwinners and women as homemakers, women still earn, on average, only about 83 percent of what men earn in the same occupation. This is up significantly from 1960 when women earned about 60 percent as much as men. The fact that women's pay still lags behind that of men, despite the passage of employment laws, is very troubling.

Donald Trump defeated Hillary Clinton for the presidency.
Many believed the nation wasn't ready for a female president.

Generations of continued inequality gave rise to today's women's movement. It's often called the third wave of feminism. The heated political climate during the 2016 election fanned the flames of the movement. Former secretary of state and first lady Hillary Clinton ran against real estate businessman Donald Trump. Many women felt demeaned by comments Trump made during his presidential campaign. They worried that, if elected, his views about women and thus his policies might set the women's movement back.

Many people also believed it was high time a woman became president. This was a big change from back in 1960. Then, a Gallup poll was conducted, asking women if they approved of the idea of a female president. Two-thirds of women did not approve. Fifty-six years later, Hillary Clinton won the popular vote (the total number of votes cast). But she lost the Electoral College vote. Each state is given a number of votes that matches that state's number of congressional representatives and senators. The Electoral College vote is the one that counts, so Trump was elected the 45th president of the United States. As in any election,

The day after Donald Trump's inauguration, women all over the world marched for women's rights.

some people were frustrated with the outcome.

On November 9, 2016, the day after the election, a woman named Teresa Shook took to social media with an idea. She suggested a women's march on Washington to voice women's concerns with the incoming administration. The Facebook post spread quickly. Women across the globe were immediately interested. Social media gave the movement a huge voice and reach. In contrast, in the days before the Internet, the NOW organizers of the 1970 march couldn't physically answer the vast numbers of handwritten letters wanting to know more about their movement. With social media, the 2017 Women's March organizers could post details in a matter of minutes and reach millions.

Eventually Bob Bland, Tamika Mallory, Carmen Perez, and Linda Sarsour organized a massive march in Washington, D.C., the day after the presidential inauguration. On January 21, 2017, event organizers estimated more than one million marchers took to Washington's streets. Additionally, they estimated nearly 5 million people—women, men, and children—marched in 673 sister marches throughout the nation and all over the world.

They chanted and waved signs including "Women's Rights are Human Rights," and "Girls Just Wanna Have Fundamental Rights."

Today's marchers still fight for equal pay and unrestricted abortion rights. But the goals of the modern women's movement are broader than those of the earlier movements. Their guiding

WOMEN WEAR WHITE

Clothing has served as important symbols of the women's movement over the years. In the first wave of feminism, women often wore white to symbolize purity and the struggle for the vote. In a nod to the suffragists, Hillary Clinton wore all white to the third presidential debate. Democratic women wore white and sat together to make a statement during President Trump's first congressional address on February 28, 2017. During the third wave of feminism, pink hats were all the rage. Directions to make the hats were available on the march organizers' website. Since pink is a color often associated with women, the hats represented women standing up for their rights.

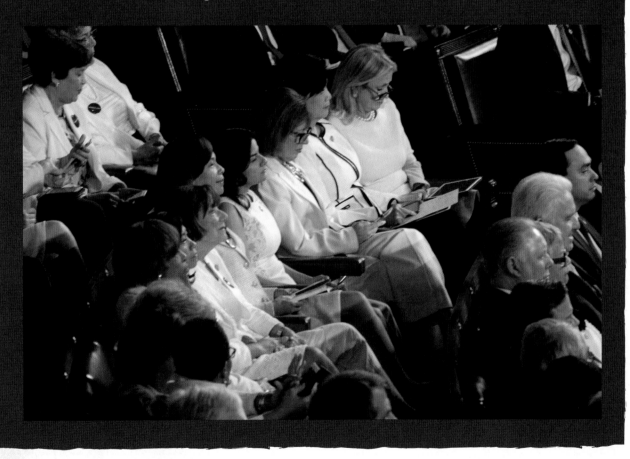

principles state "women's rights are human rights and human rights are women's rights." Today's movement includes the fight for racial justice, gay and transgender rights, and rights for those with disabilities.

The 2016 election and the Women's March on Washington allowed society to reflect on what has been achieved in the last 50 years, but it also spotlighted the inequality that remains and the way women who speak up and demand change are stigmatized.

Hillary Clinton was interrupted and called a "nasty woman" by her opponent in the third presidential debate while she spoke about Social Security and taxes.

Many believe that sexism was one of the main reasons Hillary Clinton lost the 2016 presidential election.

Senator Kamala Harris of California is one of the many women in government who have started to make their voices heard—on both sides of the aisle.

This treatment demonstrated a double standard that still runs deep in our society: men can speak their minds freely, but women must be polite.

Yet if women's voices are truly to be heard then more women need to be in decision-making roles in government. And they need to be allowed to do their jobs just like their male colleagues. But women who speak up and demand answers often find themselves silenced. Democratic Senator Kamala Harris was reprimanded by her male colleagues for demanding direct answers in a 2017 Senate Intelligence Committee hearing. But male senators who were equally blunt were not expected to act ladylike.

Massachusetts Senator Elizabeth Warren was prohibited from speaking during a Senate nomination debate. She had just quoted from a letter by Coretta Scott King, the widow of Martin Luther King Jr. The letter had already been admitted into the Senate record, but Warren was accused of calling into question the character of the nominee. So Senator Warren was forced to remain silent for the rest of the debate.

Senate Majority Leader Mitch McConnell said of Warren, **"She was warned. She was given an explanation. Nevertheless, she persisted."**

So, too, the women's movement will persist. It will march forward. Boldly. Bravely. Persistently. With heads held high and loud unladylike voices demanding to be heard.

TIMELINE

July 19-20, 1848—Woman's Rights Convention

1916—Margaret Sanger opens the first birth control clinic in the U.S.

1920—19th Amendment gives women the right to vote

1923—Alice Paul authors the Equal Rights Amendment

1953—Gregory Pincus receives funding to develop "the pill"

1961—President Kennedy forms Presidential Commission on the Status of Women

1963—Equal Pay Act becomes law

Sept. 7, 1968—Protesters disrupt Miss America pageant

March 18, 1970—Staffers take over *Ladies' Home Journal*

August 26, 1970—Thousands march in the Strike for Equality

1972—Title IX of Educational Amendments Act is signed into law

1973—*Roe v. Wade* makes abortion legal in the U.S.

Sept. 20, 1973—Tennis great Billie Jean King wins the "battle of the sexes" against Bobby Riggs

1974—Depository Institutions Amendments Act becomes law

1978—Pregnancy Discrimination Act becomes law

1982—The Equal Rights Amendment fails to get 38 states to ratify it

1991—Anita Hill testifies at Clarence Thomas' confirmation hearing

Jan. 21, 2017—Millions participate in the Women's March on Washington and around the world

GLOSSARY

breadwinner—a person whose wages support his or her family

contraceptive—a device or medication used to prevent pregnancy

degrade—to make a person feel useless or bad about himself or herself

feminist—person who believes strongly that women ought to have the same opportunities and rights that men have

fetus—an unborn human

gender—the behavioral, cultural, or psychological traits typically associated with one sex

obscene—repulsive or disgusting; shocking to one's sense of what is decent

post-traumatic stress disorder—condition experienced by soldiers or civilians who survive catastrophic events

segregation—practice of separating people of different races, income classes, gender, or ethnic groups

stigma—a mark or feeling of shame

suffragist—a supporter of women's right to vote

transgender—a person whose sense of self and gender differ from the sex assigned at birth

READ MORE

Fabiny, Sara**h**. *Who Is Gloria Steinem?* New York: Grosset & Dunlap, 2014.

Markel, Michelle**.** *Hillary Rodham Clinton: Some Girls Are Born to Lead.* New York: Balzer & Bray, 2016

Nardo, Don**.** *The Split History of the Women's Suffrage Movement: A Perspectives Flip Book.* Mankato, Minn.: Compass Point Books, 2014.

CRITICAL THINKING QUESTIONS

1. How does a middle-class woman's life in 1960 compare to a modern middle-class woman's life? Create a Venn diagram to show similarities and differences.
2. How does access to contraception affect a woman's ability to support herself? Cite evidence from the text.
3. Is the Equal Rights Amendment still important today or is it no longer necessary to pass the law? Support your opinion with facts gleaned from the text and other sources.

INTERNET SITES

Use FactHound to find internet sites related to this book.

Visit *www.facthound.com*

Just type in 9781543503869 and go.

ABOUT THE AUTHOR

Rebecca Langston-George is an elementary school teacher and the author of several books for children including *For the Right to Learn: Malala Yousafzai's Story*, a National Network of State Teachers of the Year recommended title. The California Reading Association presented her with the 2016 Armin Schulz Literary Award for a writer whose books promote social justice. Rebecca volunteers as the assistant regional advisor for the Society of Children's Writers and Illustrators (SCBWI) Central-Coastal region. You can read more at http://www.rebeccalangston-george.com

INDEX